THE COMPANION GUIDE TO
A HIGH IMPACT LIFE

HIGH IMPACT HABITS

Pete Ochs

TABLE OF CONTENTS

We are what we repeatedly do. Excellence, then, is not an act but a habit.

Aristotle

Welcome to the Study

Welcome to High Impact Habits. Our hope is that this study will equip, encourage, and inspire you to great personal transformation; a LIFE that is truly centered on living for something greater than yourself. Our goal over the next eight lessons is to challenge you to become a person disciplined in exercising three life-changing HIGH IMPACT HABITS. These habits are neither difficult nor time consuming, but it is essential that they become a part of how you live LIFE daily. Let's take a look at an overview of the three habits.

1. Life Plan Habit
KNOW where you are going.

We will help you develop a LIFE PLAN that will define your Purpose, discover your Passions, and leverage your Platform. We will challenge you to think strategically and embrace accountability. You will also learn how to use several High Impact tools to help you accomplish your God-given calling in life. This habit will entail an annual planning session and four quarterly accountability sessions.

2. Weekly Strategy Habit
BELIEVE where you are going.

We will teach you how to complete a WEEKLY STRATEGY that will allow you to maximize your impact by prioritizing the important over the urgent and develop a rhythm to your week. This will be driven by three key tools: Your annual LIFE PLAN, your TO DO list, and your weekly CALENDAR. This habit will take approximately thirty minutes of time each week and will be summarized on your WEEKLY STRATEGY SHEET.

3. Daily Execution Habit
DO what you have planned.

A DAILY EXECUTION habit that will build focus and accountability for living with high impact. This habit will focus on your daily rhythm and ensure that each day includes activities that lead you to a life of flourishing with sufficient material provision, deep authentic relationships, and a defined purpose for living.

STUDY FORMAT

Each week the study will challenge you to **KNOW**, to **BELIEVE**, and to **DO**.

KNOW – Each week you will invest in yourself by reading, watching, and participating in activities that will challenge you to change the way you think. We have made your participation in this process very simple. Besides having a copy of *A High Impact LIFE* book and this study guide, you will simply need to use the web link or QR code beside each exercise which will take you to the content you need. All of this content has been curated to help you Love your Purpose, Live with Passion, and Leverage your Platform. Our goal is to challenge you spiritually, socially, and economically with the purpose of helping you flourish.

BELIEVE – As you invest in yourself through these various activities, we also want to inspire you to become a person of great faith. A full head and an empty heart usually result in arrogance. A full heart and an empty head often lead to less than excellent results. Our hope is that through various exercises, deep reflection, and God's prompting, you will begin to believe in a vision for how you can live differently and with greater impact. In this section you will complete questions and exercises that hopefully inspire you to become all that God desires you to be.

DO – Many know, some believe, few do. Our desire is for you to become a person of great impact for Christ in a world that is desperate for answers. Each week we will provide you with exercises in hopes that you will begin to live out the three High Impact Habits. Over the next eight lessons you will complete a LIFE plan, master a few very powerful tools, and hopefully become excited and disciplined in exercising three simple habits that will change your LIFE.

TOOLS REQUIRED

1. **CALENDAR** – paper or electronic.

2. **TO DO LIST** – paper or electronic.

3. **LIFE JOURNAL** – a paper or electronic journal that will record notes, ideas, and important information and answers to the questions in this study.

4. **WEEKLY STRATEGY** – you will create this using the weekly strategy form.

5. **LIFE PLAN** – you will create this using the LIFE planning system.

6. **RUNNING BUDDY** – a personal accountability partner.

KEYS TO SUCCESS

This study is designed to challenge your core beliefs. If you really want to live with greater impact, then it will require you begin to think, believe and live differently. For you to maximize the impact this study will have on your LIFE, the following are essential commitments you must make.

1. Commit to being faithful in completing all assigned work, especially the required memory verses.

2. Commit to the daily practice of spending time with God and reviewing your daily execution.

3. Commit to spending 30 minutes per week in prayerful strategy.

4. Commit to completing your annual plan and quarterly reviews.

5. Commit to finish all eight lessons.

6. Commit to finding a "running buddy" accountability partner who will help you along the journey on a quarterly basis.

If taken seriously, this study will transform your LIFE. It is designed to help you Love your Purpose, Live with Passion, and Leverage your Platform. In turn, you will glorify God by using your gifts and passions to maximize your LIFE. In the end, it is our hope for the Creator of the University to greet you with those welcome words, "Well done."

Our desire is to see you grow deeper in your faith walk with Jesus, trust the Father for who He says He is, and allow the Holy Spirit to change you in ways you could never imagine. Our vision is to see you become a person of character, connection, competence, and commitment.

USING QR CODE READER

Once you have a QR Code reader installed on your smartphone, you're ready to scan your first QR Code.

1. Open the QR Code reader on your phone.

2. Hold your device over a QR Code so that it's clearly visible within your smartphone's screen. Depending on the reader, your phone may automatically scan the code or you may need to press a button

3. If necessary, press the button. Your phone reads the code and navigates your device to the intended destination.

Plan your work for today and every day, then work your plan.

Margaret Thatcher

Lesson 1

Weekly Strategy & Tools

KNOW
Our goal this week is to challenge you to question how you live life. Am I living a satisfied, fulfilled life that is having impact on the people I love and on the world in which I live?

BELIEVE
You will be challenged to ask why, define success, and begin to compare and contrast how you are actually living to how you would like to be living.

DO
You will be introduced to five important tools and complete your first weekly strategy.

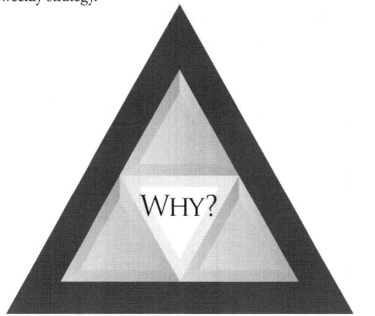

KNOW Invest in Yourself

Why do I exist? Is it to be "successful" by the world's standard or to live a life that will have eternal impact? As Socrates says, "The unexamined life is not worth living." This lesson will challenge us to examine how we are living LIFE and dive deeply into the WHY of Life. Our goal is to have you think honestly about life, success, and fulfillment. We will fast forward to the end of your life and take an honest look back at how you want to be known.

Here are your assignments for this lesson.

Memorize 1 John 2:15-16

> Do not love the world or anything in the world, for if anyone loves the world the love of the father is not in him. For everything in the world, the cravings of sinful man, the lust of his eyes, and the boasting of what he has and does comes not from the father but from the world.

Read Chapter 1 in *A High Impact LIFE*. Highlight the concepts that spoke deeply to you. Be prepared to discuss these highlights with your small group.

Watch: Dealmakers Documentary, https://vimeo.com/224524840

Read: The Implications of Calling,
Dr. Art Lindsley, https://tifwe.org/the-implications-of-calling/

Watch: God Wants Your Heart, Not Your Success, Henry Kaestner, https://www.youtube.com/watch?v=TyGFAcDI-As&list=PL9Ew9GPm-33Wq3QYnnApwYdINybrsPQWMx&index=2

BELIEVE  Be Inspired

Throughout a typical day we are barraged by the complexities of life leaving us very little time to thoughtfully consider one of the most important questions on earth. Why do I exist? Why do I strive with such vigor to only conclude at the end of the day "all is vanity?" We hope to upend your world a bit in this next section by asking you some very direct questions regarding the purpose of it all. Don't hold back, jump in and challenge yourself to think honestly and openly about your life. We would encourage you to use your life journal to record the answers to your questions and any other thoughts or ideas you may have.

Think & Reflect

1. If you died today, how would your friends and family describe your life? If they were to give an honest account, how would they describe you and the life you had lived?

2. Read Matthew 25:14-30. The parable describes two different types of lives. One that was well lived and one that wasn't. If you were to stand before your Master today, would he greet you with the words, "Well done, good and faithful servant. You have been faithful with a few things. I will put in charge of many things?"

Are you faithful in the things God has entrusted you to manage?

3. Reflect on your personal life, your family life, your job, your friendships, and your dreams. Would you say your life is fulfilled? Where do you think your life may be lacking?

4. Why doesn't success bring satisfaction and fulfillment? Or does it?

5. As discussed on page six in the section "The World of Me," most of us let the world define success for us instead of letting God's Word define success for us. Consequently, our lives are lived for ME. Do you let the world define success for you? How did you determine where to live, what kind of car to drive, and what job to have?

6. The biggest mistake we often make is that we believe our Platform (job, career, vocation) is our Purpose in life. Have you made that mistake? Why did you honestly take the job you currently have?

7. Lauren Rolph makes the statement that "Success is in Surrender." What is your first impression of that statement? Can you identify with that statement? If not, why?

8. Read 1 John 2:15-16. What are three things the Scripture says come from the world? How do those three items relate to your own life? Have you found yourself chasing Pride, Pleasure, and Possessions?

9. How much time do you spend on the "Who I am? How I live? And What I own?" questions of life?

10. Watch this video by Simon Senek.

https://bit.ly/1w2ZyO5

Have you honestly asked yourself this question, "Why do I exist?" If not, then take some time NOW and answer it. What is your answer?

11. Watch this video by Michael Jr.

https://youtu.be/LZe5y2D60YU.

Complete this phrase: When you know your _____ your _____ has more _____ because you're walking in or towards your _____.

12. So why don't we spend time thinking about the Why of life?

13. The essence of a high-impact life is to know with your head, believe with your heart, and work with your hands to fulfill the purpose, passion, and platform God has designed you for. Based on this definition of a high impact LIFE, where would you score your life on a scale of 1-10, 10 being perfect.

14. EULOGY. Write your own eulogy as if you died today. Now write a second eulogy as if you had died after living the kind of life you envision for yourself. How do the two eulogies differ? Why do you think that is?

15. What idea challenged you the most in this chapter?

DO ✋ Make an Impact

Over the next eight weeks our goal is to help you become very proficient and disciplined in exercising the three High Impact Habits. These habits will involve learning several simple tools that will transform the way you live and the impact you will have. These are simple and easy but must become a regular part of your routine. I cannot stress enough the importance of this exercise. This exercise alone will add 25-30% productivity to your life if you use it properly. Not only will you be doing the thing right, but more importantly it will help you also do the right thing. It will help you determine the urgent from the important. Remember there are three High Impact Habits:

1. LIFE Plan Habit
2. Weekly Strategy Habit
3. Daily Execution Habit

All of these are necessary and nonnegotiable habits and they do not have to be done in the order of the habit. They each need to be done in concert with the other and more importantly must truly become a HABIT and not a one-time exercise. That said, we will start with the WEEKLY STRATEGY HABIT. We are starting with this habit first because we only have eight lessons together and it will make the most sense and provide you the best accountability if we start with the Weekly Strategy. Next week we will address Daily Execution and the following six weeks we will focus on the LIFE Plan because of the depth of that process.

To effectively execute on a WEEKLY STRATEGY, you will need to understand the following:

TOOLS

Journal – I am a big believer in using a journal, either a physical notebook or electronic version, that will allow you to keep a running log of all you do. This might include one each for personal and professional notations. In fact, I carry two with me: one for personal and one for business. I prefer a Moleskine journal (5 x 8.25). I will record meeting notes, ideas, sketches, sermon notes, names of people, etc. Since I don't use an electronic notebook, I will often take a picture with my phone of the pages that I would like to file and then archive them electronically using a system such as Evernote on my computer.

Often times when recording information, it triggers an action item that I need or simply want to do. On the outside margin of my journal, I will make a square box indicating that this needs further attention. This could include adding something to my TO DO List, electronically filing a note, or some other form of action. Once I have completed that action, I put a check mark in the box noting that it has been completed.

As I go through the day I simply record notes starting in the front of my journal and record them in sequential order. If you use an electronic journal, be sure and use one that will stand the test of time and will allow you to keep files active on any computer platform for the next 50 years. Also, use one that will allow you to add topics to your journal thoughts. I often times write or record information on a particular topic, and it will be very helpful to have the ability to go back and sort all of your notes by topic. Doing so will help you to develop your philosophy of life that is more easily shared with others.

Here is a copy of a page out of my business journal.

Summit Overview

Follow up with Keynote speakers

Check in with team on paperwork to vendors

Coordinatey with E.M. & D.J. On Invite List

Approve list 2-1 // 100 Names

What does physical versus digital invitation

look like?

Personal outreach versus mass mailing

Day planning, minute by minute breakdown

To Do List – Most of us already use TO DO lists and many of you already have a system for managing your to do list. If this is the case, great. Keep using this system if it already works for you. If you don't have a TO DO list or if it is haphazard and scattered (i.e. sticky notes and small pieces of paper scattered everywhere), here are a couple of suggestions. You can use a to do list on your smart phone or you can do what I do and keep your TO DO list in the back of your journal. Whatever system works for you is the best to use. Just make sure you have a TO DO list and it is always up to date.

If you are using your journal for your TO DO list, this is what I would recommend. Start in the back of your journal and start recording your TO DOs. On the left-hand margin of my TO DO list I leave enough space for various symbols that allow me to understand various information about each item. Below is a listing of my symbols and what they mean

o (Check mark) – means the item has been completed.

o (Arrow) – means I have delegated the item to someone else and I will put their name beside the arrow

o (circle) – means I have started to work on the item but there is more to do, I have delegated the items and it needs follow-up, or I need additional information to finish it up.

o (A, B, C) - I will often times write an A, B, or C on the RIGHT side of the page, so I can categorize the importance of the to do item. A's are the most important.

Over time my list will become quite jumbled with new to dos, completed to dos, and in process to dos. Whenever this happens and I feel it is becoming unwieldy, I simply draw a line and bring forward all my unfinished items. This takes a little bit of time, but I have found that this exercise will often times allow me to drop to do's that I thought were important a few weeks ago but for some reason aren't important today.

Here is a copy of my TO DO list.

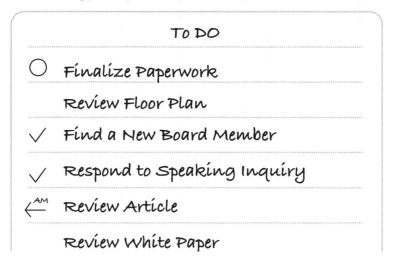

Calendar – Most of us now use the calendars in our smart phones and this is great. If you don't do this, then make sure you have some type of calendar to record your appointments and important dates. This calendar should be kept with you at all times so that you have a real time navigation tool to plan your LIFE.

Life Plan – If you have an annual personal plan, then you can use it. If not, the good news is that within a few weeks you will have a plan if you stay faithful in completing this study. For now, we will not worry about the annual plan but that will be coming in the next few weeks.

HIGH IMPACT HABIT

Weekly Strategy – It's time to learn your first new habit, so let's jump right in. Each week you will need to designate approximately 30 minutes for your weekly strategy time. It can be anytime of the week, but I prefer Sunday evening because I am well rested, my mind is clear, it is usually a quiet time around the house, I am not traveling, and it is the first of the week. Here are the key steps you need to complete during this time so that your weekly strategy session becomes a very powerful habit.

1. Draw in your journal or print a copy of the WEEKLY STRATEGY Document.

2. I simply draw out eight squares on a complete page in my journal and use this as the planning tool. You can also print these and keep them as loose leafs in your journal. The eight squares represent one square for each day of the week plus one extra square where you can record everyday items such as compliment your spouse, exercise,

read, etc.

3. Review your calendar and write the time and meeting topic for each meeting you have this week on the WEEKLY STRATEGY Sheet. It is absolutely critical to understand your own personal rhythm when scheduling meetings. I simply will not schedule any meetings before noon because I want to reserve the most efficient part of the day (morning for me) for the tasks which I need to accomplish. Therefore, I only schedule meetings in the afternoon. You will need to determine what is your best rhythm for the tasks you need to accomplish.

4. Review your TO DO list. This is a critical component to your success. Prioritize the most important things to do with the letter A. Write these TO DO items that you want to accomplish THIS WEEK into your WEEKLY STRATEGY sheet scheduling them when you are most efficient. After you have scheduled in the A items, you can fill in with the less important B & C items.

5. Review your LIFE plan, particularly your Goals and Action Items. This is important because it will force you to do the important over the urgent. Once again it is critical that you schedule time each week to help you meet your personal goals. I will often schedule 2-4 hours per week for personal improvement, exercise, etc.

6. And lastly, on your WEEKLY STRATEGY, be sure and leave time throughout each day for unexpected projects and meetings that require time you had not allocated. Additionally, don't schedule things so close that if something important requires immediate attention, it will not ruin your entire schedule. Hence another reason I like scheduling meetings in the afternoon.

Here is an example of a completed weekly strategy worksheet.

Weekly Strategy INNOVATION	Date March 3 - 9
Daily Repeatable Activities	**Sunday** 3/3
6 AM TIME W/GOD AFFIRM SPOUSE	8 AM CHURCH 5 PM REVIEW ANNUAL PLAN & WEEKLY STRATEGY
Monday 3/4	**Tuesday** 3/5
12 PM BUDGET REVIEW 2PM PHONE CALLS MENTOR SESSION	FINE TUNE CONF. PLAN 11 AM PLAN SESSION 6 PM RUNNING BUDDY
Wednesday 3/6	**Thursday** 3/7
11 AM MANG. MTGS 12 PM LEADERSHIP LUNCH MTG W/ P. ROLPH MTG W/ JON MTG W/JEFF	11 AM REVISE WHITE PAPER PHONE CALLS 1 PM MENTOR MTG 3 PM TA BD MTG
Friday 3/8	**Saturday** 3/9
2 PM FINISH WHITEPAPER 4 PM END OF WEEK 7 PM BBALL GAME	10 AM HOUSE TO DO'S 2PM TREEHOUSE - GKIDS

SUMMARY

To summarize your practical application for this week. You will do the following:

1. Assemble your calendar, journal, and TO DO list.

2. Determine a time when you have 30 minutes to strategize your week.

3. Download a copy of the WEEKLY STRATEGY SHEET or simply draw the boxes in your journal page. Download here: https://bit.ly/2U0ovOg

4. Strategize your week using the weekly strategy worksheet. Synthesize the information in your calendar, your TO DO list, and your LIFE Plan (not completed yet but coming soon).

5. Each morning before you start the day, review your WEEKLY STRATEGY SHEET so that you can maximize your efforts throughout the day. DO NOT VIOLATE YOUR PLAN UNLESS IT IS ABSOLUTELY IMPERATIVE. If you find that you are not following your WEEKLY STRATEGY, then you are either very undisciplined or you are not doing a good job of prioritizing and strategizing your week.

Visit go.enterprisestewardship.com/annual-plan and download the free Downloadable LIFE Plan. We will use this plan over the next several weeks so keep it handy.

An honest heart is the first blessing, a knowing head is the second.

Thomas Jefferson

Lesson 2

Daily Execution

KNOW

Our goal this week is for you to understand the importance of knowing your purpose and introduce you to determining your passions and leveraging your platform.

BELIEVE

You will be challenged to choose surrender over success.

DO

You will be introduced to the second High Impact Habit: Daily Execution.

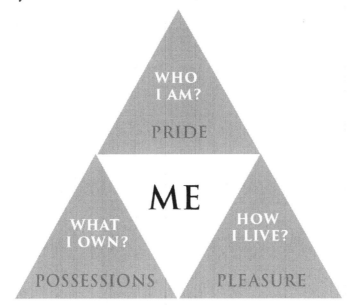

KNOW Invest in Yourself

A.W. Tozer said, "It is not what a man does that determines whether his work is sacred or secular; it is why he does it." Answering the "why?" question is the calibration to your life. It is essential for both personal and professional growth. A correct answer to the "Why?" question allows you to set your sights on a greater purpose than yourself. This new purpose is born out of a transformed life. Simply put, a transformed life is trading in your pride, pleasure, and possessions for something greater: service, excellence, and stewardship.

Many people do not take the time or energy to question the why of life. On the other hand, there are those who have searched, found, and chosen the narrow road of a transformed life. However, these individuals learned quickly this road will require much sacrifice and dedication. We invite you to join those who have walked down the journey of a transformed life and to take a bold stand to live for the glory of God!

Here are your assignments for this lesson.

Memorize Galatians 2:20

> I have been crucified with Christ. It is no longer I who live but Christ lives in me. And the life I now live in the flesh I live by faith in the Son of God, who loved me and gave himself for me.

Read Chapter 2 in *A High Impact LIFE*. Highlight the concepts that spoke deeply to you. Be prepared to discuss these highlights with your small group.

Read: What it Means to Be a Leader of No Reputation
Dr. Scott Rodin, http://thestewardsjourney.com/
what-it-means-to-be-a-leader-of-no-reputation/

Read: The Difference Between Calling and Work
Hugh Whelchel, https://tifwe.org/the-difference-
between-calling-and-work/

Read: The Ambition Explosion
David Brooks, https://www.nytimes.com/2014/11/28/
opinion/david-brooks-the-ambition-explosion.html

BELIEVE  Be Inspired

In chapter one we spent most of our time asking ourselves difficult questions to challenge us to truly understand the why of life. In this lesson we are going to try and finalize some thoughts on your purpose and then discuss how our purpose determines our passions. When I live for myself with ME as the head of my Kingdom, my passions will typically revolve around pride (or position), pleasure, and possessions. If I surrender to the Creator of the Universe and understand the potential for impact that this will have on my life, my passions will turn to service, excellence, and stewardship.

The ultimate form of surrender is for us to embrace the words of Paul when he said, "I have been crucified with Christ and I no longer live but Christ lives in me. The life I live in the body I live by FAITH in the Son of God who loved me and gave Himself for me." Our challenge for this week is to embrace surrender and understand the power of a surrendered life.

1. After reading Chapter 2, are you honestly satisfied with the impact you are having on the people around you, the community you live in, and the country you love? If no, what areas of your life do you need to make changes in?

2. As Christians, the tension to live a surrendered life is even more pronounced because that is what Christ has called us to do. Often times as Christians "we spread a little Christian frosting in the form of feigned humility or self serving generosity on our cardboard lives to make us think all is well, but inside we are hollow and unfilled." Is this you? If so, what are the things in your life that keep you from living a life of complete surrender to God's will?

3. Are you truly living for a cause greater than yourself and if so, how would you describe that cause?

4. If we are truly living to glorify God and enjoy him forever, I believe there are several questions that will help us examine our lives. For each question below, provide an honest answer. If the answer is "NO", then spend some time determining why.

   a. Do I love people unconditionally?

   b. Do I work diligently at all I do both professionally and personally?

   c. Do I live a simple unfettered life?

   d. Do I risk my time, talent, and treasure for the cause of Christ?

   e. Do I give generously?

5. Paul says in Galatians 2:20, "I have been crucified with Christ

and I no longer live but Christ lives in me." What does it mean to you to be "crucified with Christ?"

6. Passion is a powerful thing. What are you passionate about? Do your passions determine how you live or are they something that reside in your dreams?

7. Read Psalm 139:14. What talents or abilities has God blessed you with? How are you utilizing those skills in your family, workplace, or community? Is there any part of you that is holding back? Why or why not?

8. Your purpose determines your passion. If our new found purpose is to glorify God and enjoy him forever, then our new found passions should be to serve people, pursue excellence, and be a good steward of all that God has given us to manage. If you were to rate yourself in each of these three areas, how would you describe your current behavior in each area?

    a. Service to others?

    b. The pursuit of excellence in all you do?

    c. The stewardship of your time, talent, treasure, and tribe?

9. Do you feel a deep satisfaction, contentment, and joy in the work God has called you to do? Explain why or why not. Is God calling you to change your platform (current job, vocation, or career)?

10. Do you have a strong vision for how God can use you in your current vocation? If not, what do you see as the hindrances to making this happen?

11. The LIFE acrostic stands for Labor, Influence, Financial Resources, and Expertise. How well are you stewarding these resources in light of the fact that we all want to be greeted at heaven's gate with the salutation, "Well done, good and faithful servant." Comment on each of the four areas.

12. 2 Timothy 1:7 says: "God has not given us a spirit of timidity, but a spirit of power, of love and of self-discipline." Write a short paragraph describing the current state of your spirit as it relates to the challenge provided us in this verse.

13. Take some time to define your purpose, passion, and platform. Ask yourself: are you loving your purpose, living with passion, and leveraging your platform?

14. Living a High Impact LIFE demands that life change occurs with daily action and accountability. Think about one area in your life that you are not satisfied with. What is one action step you can take today in order to achieve the goals you have with your purpose, passion, and platform? How will you measure this? Who will keep you accountable?

DO ✋ Impact your World

High Impact Habit – Daily Execution

In our last lesson we learned the habit of the Weekly Strategy. This consisted of looking at your calendar for the coming week, your to do list, and your annual plan and then strategizing what your upcoming week should look like. As you determine your WEEKLY STRATEGY it's importance to align your personal rhythm with the tasks you need to accomplish. This is a very powerful habit and will provide you with great focus and efficiency over the week. But to make this habit very impactful, you must execute on a daily basis. These are the essential things you should do on a daily basis.

1. Daily Routine. Establish an everyday morning and evening routine. We cannot overemphasize the importance of a morning routine that allocates your morning hours to your most important duties. These include time with God, time for reflection and planning, and time to accomplish the items that require the most focused mental attention. Save less important items such as checking email, meetings, and phone calls for right before or after lunch.

2. Review Weekly Strategy. Review your weekly strategy worksheet daily to keep you on track. During your morning time of reflection, a quick review of the Weekly Strategy Worksheet you completed on Sunday night will ensure that your most important TO DOs are at the forefront of your mind to start the day. I like to start with the task that will allow me to have the highest impact. Unfortunately, these are often the tasks that are the least appealing to do. But be disciplined and do the important over the urgent.

3. Time Allocation. Allow sufficient time during the day to complete the most important tasks. It's important that you become adept at allocating the proper amount of time to complete a task. My biggest problem in life is that I am too optimistic as to the length of time it takes to accomplish something and to complete it with excellence.

4. Discipline. Be very disciplined in personal habits. Try to go to bed in the evening with a mind that has been cleared of the cares and worries of the day. This can be accomplished in a number of ways, but leaving work at work is a good start. Stay away from the TV and other screens right before you go to bed. Instead, fill your mind with inspirational thoughts from Scripture or other positive and virtuous media.

You now have acquired the knowledge to become proficient in the first two High Impact Habits. **Weekly Strategy** and **Daily Execution.** As you can see, both are quite simple to do. The key is **Doing** them! Let's do a quick review.

SUMMARY

To recap the concept of your WEEKLY STRATEGY, here is your checklist:

One time per week find 30 minutes of quiet time when your head and heart are clear from the clutters of the world.

Assemble and review your JOURNAL, your TO DO list, your CALENDAR, and your LIFE PLAN.

Using all the information in these tools, strategize your upcoming week. Remember, do the important, not the urgent. Give the best part of your day to God and then yourself. Allow sufficient time between duties. Review this daily to make sure you are on track.

DAILY EXECUTION. Review your Weekly Strategy Sheet, be disciplined in your daily routine, allow for a specific time to do the mundane, and focus on the important not the urgent.

I thank God for my handicaps for, through them, I have found myself, my work, and my God.

Helen Keller

Lesson 3

LIFE Plan - Purpose - Values

KNOW

You will be challenged to Honor God as the PURPOSE for your life.

BELIEVE

You will learn the three virtues of Truth, Faith, and Character that will allow you to Honor God in a very powerful way.

DO

You will review the Weekly Strategy and Daily Execution Habits and complete the Purpose section of your Personal Plan.

KNOW 🗣 Invest in Yourself

Why do I exist? To honor God. You might know this answer or at least have heard it taught before. However, to get this phrase from your head to your heart and into your life will take a process of obedience. You see we are born with a problem. This problem puts us at the center of our life and whether we would like to admit it or not, we think everything and everyone else should honor us. This causes us to approach God with a very consumer mindset. As we approach our relationship with God, we often look to how we can benefit. While God gives many benefits and blessing (Romans 8:32), truly honoring God requires us to approach Him with a different mindset. We trade in our focus on me to a focus on Him.

Let's break this down further. This week you will discover there are three components to honoring God. These three components are broken into three categories: truth, faith, and character. Truth is to know; it's a head thing. Faith is to believe; it's a heart thing. And Character is to do; it's a hands thing.

Living with great impact requires us to know God but to also make Him known. Some would call this "being" and "doing". This lesson will focus on the "being" part or the knowing God part of our relationship with Him.

Here are your assignments for this lesson.

Memorize Matthew 22:37

> And He said to him, "You shall love the Lord with all our heart and with all your soul and will all your mind."

Read Chapter 3 in *A High Impact LIFE*. Highlight the concepts that spoke deeply to you. Be prepared to discuss these highlights with your small group.

Read: Why Loving God with All Your Mind Matters
Dr. Art Lindsley, https://tifwe.org/why-loving-god-with-all-your-mind-matters/

Read: Making It without Faking It
Jacqueline Isaacs, https://tifwe.org/making-it-without-faking-it/

Watch: Four Qualities for Enduring Leadership, Crawford Loritts, https://vimeo.com/237925258

BELIEVE ♡ Be Inspired

In chapter two we took time to discuss our purpose in life and how our purpose ultimately determines our passions. In this lesson, we are going to delve into our highest purpose which is to live and make choices in our lives that honor God.

We honor God by adhering to truth in the scriptures today. Truth is a virtue that is being replaced by feelings. We honor God by being people of faith, believing with action. We'll reflect on how we are exercising our faith and how we can grow in this area. We honor God by being a person of character, as exemplified by Christ. We'll reflect on the choices we make and how they determine our high and low points in life.

Our challenge in this lesson is to wrestle with questions that will lead us to see how we can live a surrendered LIFE instead of a "successful" life.

1. John 15:5 lays out explicitly how we can have lives of great impact. "I am the vine, you are the branches. If you remain in me and I remain in you, you will bear much fruit." Are you bearing fruit and if so, what does it look like? How do you remain in Christ?

2. Remaining in Christ is often associated with "abiding" or "being" in Christ. It is that deep personal relationship we have with God the Father through Jesus Christ. Bearing fruit often means "doing" good works in the name of Jesus. Are you an "abider" or a "doer"? Is it possible to have one without the other? Are you experiencing the joy of both being and doing?

3. Honoring God requires the pursuit of truth (knowing), faith (believing) and character (doing). Which one of these three is the easiest for you to engage in? Which is the most difficult? If you were to view these three virtues as spokes on a wheel, would you roll through life smoothly or with a fair amount of bumps?

4. Watch Metaethics: Crash Course Philosophy https://youtu.be/FOoffXFpAlU. Does it matter that you have a philosophy of life? If yes, how would you describe yours? Are you a person who believes in absolutes or are you more relative in your

belief system? Can you defend your philosophy of life?

5. "Many people know the truth, some people believe the truth, few people live out the truth." What category would you put yourself in? Why is it so difficult to live out what we know and believe to be the truth?

6. If Truth is a critical ingredient to a High Impact LIFE, please comment on how you are doing in the four essential factors that will help you find the Truth.

> a. God's Word. Spending time daily in God's word reading, studying it and memorizing it. Joshua 1:8, Psalm 119:9-11, 1 Timothy 4:13, 1 Timothy 2:15
>
> b. A growing and passionate relationship with Jesus. John 14:6
>
> c. Wise Counsel. Using others to help sharpen your saw. Proverbs 15:22
>
> d. God's created world. Daily admiring and thanking God for the miraculous world we live in. Romans 1:20

7. Often times when we are walking by faith our expectation is that God will change our circumstances to meet our needs. But His usual practice is to change us to fit his timing and circumstances. Have you experienced how God uses circumstances to change us and not our circumstance? What did you learn in this process?

8. Exercising faith requires a step. When God decides that something needs to be done, he often looks for who will get it done instead of how to get it done. What do you do and how do you live so that if God asks you to do something, you will hear His voice and

respond.

9. Exercising faith often results in a wilderness experience. Can you describe a time you have been in a "wilderness"? How can you best prepare for a coming wilderness experience? Do you embrace difficulties or run from them?

10. If our pursuit of faith is measured to some degree by our prayer life, how is your prayer life? What keeps you from being the prayer warrior you would like to be?

11. If Character is doing what you know and believe to be true, how are you doing? Do you consistently choose character over compromise?

12. Graph your life. On a sheet of paper, draw a graph. The y axis will be a measure of good times versus bad times. Good will be at the top and bad will be at the bottom and 0 or neutral will be in the middle of the axis. Starting at 0 on the Y axis (middle of graph) draw the X axis. The measurement for the X axis will be the amount of time you have been alive. Now plot the following two lines on the graph starting when you were young and moving on to where you are today. *(See example on how to set up on the next page.)*

> a. Plot the major highs (good happenings) in your life and plot the major lows (bad happenings) in your life. Connect these with a continuous line starting on the left and going right.
>
> b. Next plot your spiritual highs and lows on the same time scale. Start at 0 (birth). Plot the times when you were growing spiritually (above the 0 on the X axis) and plot the

times you were not growing or even backsliding spiritually (below the X axis line).

c. Is there any correlation to the happenings in your life (both good and bad) to your spiritual growth?

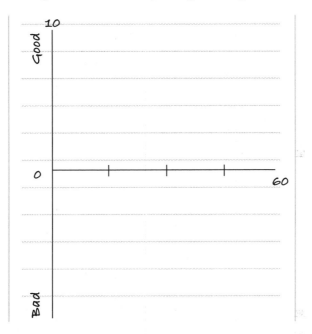

13. If our pursuit of Truth is measured by how much time we spend reading and meditating on God's Word, and if our pursuit of faith is measured by the time we spend on our knees in fervent prayer, and if our pursuit of character is measured by our obedience to God's commands, how are you doing ………

In pursuing Truth?

In pursuing Faith?

In pursuing Character?

Which of the above pursuits cause you the greatest concern and what can you do to correct this?

DO ✋ Impact your World

Weekly Strategy Habit. By now you should have completed several weeks of the Weekly Strategy Worksheet.

1. How is it going? Are you faithful in completing it weekly?
2. How well have you been able to stay on task and accomplish what you had planned to do?
3. Are you keeping your TO DO list current?
4. Are you using your journal to record meetings, notes, ideas?

Daily Execution Habit. By now you should have completed at least one week of Daily Execution Planning. Remember, the key to making this habit work is to ensure you are following a daily routine. You must begin and end everyday with the routine that prepares your heart and mind for the day ahead. Are you:

1. Spending time at the very beginning of the day with God?
2. Are you reviewing your Weekly Strategy on a daily basis to make sure you are staying on task for the day and the week?
3. At the end of the day are you reviewing the day and making mental notes as to what went well and what didn't go so well?

ANNUAL PERSONAL PLAN

OK, let's jump right in and start to create your own personal plan. This is where the rubber meets the road. I cannot overemphasize the importance of this next section. Many people know, some people believe, few people do. You are about to become one of the few "doers" who truly make an impact on this world – making the jump from doing whatever comes naturally to living intentionally.

You can download the personal plan at https://www.enterprisestewardship.com/annual-plan or go page 94 in this book.

Personal Plan Overview You are about to begin one of the most important exercises of your lifetime: creating your own Personal Plan. To make this as easy and seamless as possible, we have divided your Personal Plan work into three parts. Each part follows – and corresponds directly to – a major section of the High Impact LIFE book: Purpose, Passion, or Platform.

This Personal Plan will help you strategically and tactically implement the virtues you have been learning in this book – taking

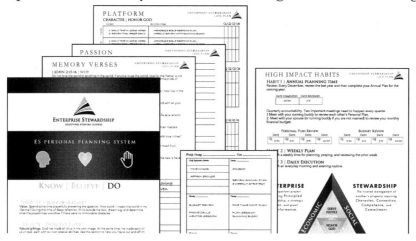

them from abstract theory to practical implementation. If you merely acknowledge the Personal Plan's value (knowing) but fail to actually implement it yourself (believing and doing) , you will have wasted your time. If, on the other hand, you invest the time – even as an experiment based on partial faith because of the testimony of others (believing) – you will experience (doing) the power of new, beneficial habits replacing old habits that may be comfortable but are holding you back.

Personal transformation starts with changing your thinking. You must fill your head with truth (knowing). Economic, social, and spiritual truth will combine to build faith (believing) that a high-impact LIFE is not only a possibility but a probability. And not just for someone else, but for you! As you begin to trust and apply the truth (doing), you become a person of great character, connection, competence, and commitment. You will become a person of high impact.

Your Personal Plan does not need to be complicated. In fact, the simpler it is, the more likely you will follow through and get the encouragement of early progress. Your plan will help you:

1. Embrace a PURPOSE for your LIFE.

2. Uncover your PASSION about who you are and how God made you.

3. Strategically develop goals and actions that will leverage your PLATFORM.

We will guide you through the two necessary steps for achieving transformation: planning and execution. Planning without execution is a daydream. Execution without planning is a nightmare. It takes both working in tandem to achieve maximum results.

Planning: The first step toward living a high-impact LIFE is to create a plan that addresses your purpose, your passion, and your platform. We are about to start that process.

Execution: The second step toward a high-impact LIFE is to execute your plan. Execution is a result of mastering the three high-impact habits. These habits are:

PERSONAL LIFE PLAN
WEEKLY STRATEGY
DAILY EXECUTION

Over the last few weeks we have focused on teaching you the last two habits: Weekly Strategy and Daily Execution. Without those your plan will become a dust-covered monument to big dreams but no impact.

Personal Plan - Love Your Purpose

The key to the LIFE Plan is the personal plan template. Included with this study is a downloadable LIFE plan template. You may also have a set of physical planning cards. Once completed, these will become your LIFE plan.

If you would like additional copies or would like to fill them out on paper before you transfer them to the cards, go to **go.enterprisestewardship.com/annual-plan** or use the QR code to the right to download the LIFE planning document titled LIFE Plan.

Over the next few minutes we are going to step you through several exercises that will help you create, confirm and begin to embrace your PURPOSE in life. The first part of your LIFE Plan will define your purpose in life. In this section, we will seek to identify and help you understand your God-glorifying purpose. Now that you have the LIFE Plan document in hand, let's begin to complete the Purpose section.

Purpose – Why do I exist?

Vision. Spend some time prayerfully answering the question: How could I impact the world in my lifetime? During this time of deep reflection, think outside the box, dream big, and determine what the possibilities would be if there were no obstacles.

Action Item: Spend time journaling and recording ideas for your purpose statement. It may include your various roles as a Christian, a spouse, a parent, and a member of society. Think about how you can change the world you live in, beginning with your current sphere of influence and working toward what you can envision it becoming. Try to get your purpose statement down to two or three sentences. Here is my Purpose statement to give you an idea of what it could look like. "I want to know Christ and make Him known by being a loving husband, available father, faithful friend, and an enterprise steward. I will impact the world for Christ by serving with excellence as I steward the capital God has given me." When you are satisfied with yours, record it in your LIFE Plan document. Now, memorize it.

Values. Think carefully about the values or character traits that you believe would make you a steward of great reputation. Choose four to six of them for your personal focus. These values will become part of your core identity, how people think of you. Keep them short and simple, preferably a word or two for each so that they remain top of mind and are easily shared with others. My four personal values are: Honor God, Serve people, Pursue excellence, and Steward capital.

Action Item: Write down these values in your Personal Plan document and memorize them.

Life verse. Is there a particular Scripture that is meaningful and describes the way you want to live LIFE? If so, consider making it your life verse. If not, search for one that you could claim as your own, treating it as God's vision for your LIFE. I have had several life verses, changing them as my role has changed. You could also have several life verses, one for each of the key positions you hold: spouse, parent, job, church, etc.

Action Item: Prayerfully determine a Scripture that represents God's vision for your life. Record it in your LIFE Plan document. During the next few weeks, memorize it and repeat it often. Over time you will find it guiding you in ways you never would have thought.

Whatever you do, work heartily, as for the Lord and not for men, knowing that from the Lord you will receive the inheritance as your reward. You are serving the Lord Christ.

Colossians 3:23-24

For you are my rock and my fortress; and for your name's sake you lead me and guide me.

Psalm 31:3

SUMMARY

Okay, that wasn't so hard, was it?

Continue to think through your purpose, and don't be afraid to refine it over time.   Over the next two lessons we will tackle the Passion section of your LIFE Plan. We will delve into what you are passionate about, your God given talents, and formulate some big ideas to help you find how God can use you for His Kingdom.

Watch: Is Something Missing in your Life?
Dr. Charles Stanley
https://youtu.be/XxcEWIFRNyU

Watch: Mustard Seed Faith
 Boyd Bailey
https://www.youtube.com/
watch?v=RXDxJzgWXhM

The measure of a man's greatness is not in the number of servants he has, but the number of people he serves.

John Hague

Lesson 4

LIFE Plan - Passion
50 Year Goal

KNOW

You will be called and challenged to SERVE PEOPLE.

BELIEVE

You will learn the virtues of Vision, Humility, and Courage that will allow you to Serve People in a very powerful way.

DO

You will review the Purpose section of your LIFE Plan and then start completing the Passion section of the plan.

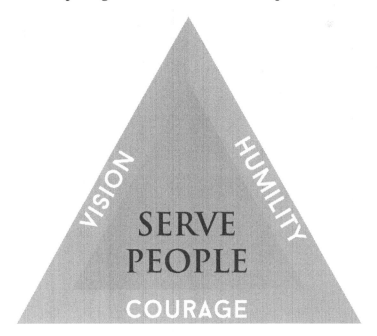

KNOW Invest in Yourself

One of the greatest ways to love our neighbor as we love ourselves is to serve them. The book of Mark tells us that Jesus came not to be served but to serve, even to the point of dying for us. We can honor God by serving others. Serving takes many forms from the simplest action of giving a quick smile or cool drink to the complex of walking through life and sharing the cares and burdens of our fellow man. It can be messy, emotional, time consuming, and at times just exhausting. But it is what we are called to do.

In this lesson we will tackle the three virtues that will help us serve people in deep and meaningful ways: vision, humility, courage. Vision shows us what should be done, humility allows us to believe that with God's help it can be done, and courage leads us to persevere until it is done.

Here are your assignments for this lesson.

Memorize Mark 10:45

> For even the Son of man came not to be served to but to serve, and to give His life as a ransom for many.

Read Chapter 4 in *A High Impact LIFE*. Highlight the concepts that spoke deeply to you. Be prepared to discuss these highlights with your small group.

Read: What it Means to Serve Others—The Mark of a Servant Leader, Christopher D. Connors, https://medium.com/the-mission/what-it-means-to-serve-others-the-mark-of-a-servant-leader-22eed3ff3fc0

Read: Why Vision Is More Important Than Strategy, Michael Hyatt, https://michaelhyatt.com/why-vision-is-more-important-than-strategy/

BELIEVE Be Inspired

In the last lesson we learned that our ultimate purpose is to honor God. In this lesson our hope is to challenge you to honor God through service to your fellow man. We hope that you will assess and reflect on the importance of vision, particularly God's vision for your life. Have you really taken time to consider how God can use you in great and mighty ways? Additionally, we will look at the importance of the virtue of humility. This is a tough one for all of us but can be the greatest hindrance to truly serving our fellow man. Lastly, we till tackle the topic of courage. Serving isn't easy, particularly if God has given you a vision that is bigger than you think you can handle in your own strength.

The lesson will challenge you to discover your what (head), why (heart), and how (hands) aspects of these three virtues and grow in how you serve the people in your life.

1. If serving is the way we exemplify our faith and is a demonstration of our devotion to Jesus, would someone who doesn't know you but observes how you live say that you are a person of deep faith and great devotion? Where could you improve your service to others?

2. Serving others is often viewed as a one-time event like handing out water bottles on a hot day or working at the school concession stand. Real service, service that has a transformational impact, requires deep commitment of your time, talent, and treasure. It's messy, emotional, and exhausting. How would you describe your current state of serving others? Is it shallow and easy or deep and transformational? Have you seen the benefits outweigh the costs?

3. Isaiah 50:4 says, "The Lord has given me the tongue of a disciple that I may know how to sustain the weary one with a word." I believe that God has given each of us the ability to be great encouragers, even to people who we have just met. Do you treat every encounter with a person as a divine appointment, a time when you can "sustain the weary one with a word?" What techniques or ideas would help you encourage your fellow man?

4. Matthew 28 exhorts us to go and make disciples of all nations. I believe that discipleship is the greatest form of serving because it is the best method for personal transformation. How are you at discipling others? Do you need to be discipled by someone? What are you going to do to become a mentor or a disciple?

5. Virtuous leaders seek to maximize the skills of those they lead by exhorting them to be people of Character, Connection, Competence, and Commitment. You might be leading your family, certain friends, fellow church members, or business associates. How would you describe your virtuous leadership skills based on the 4 C's

noted above? What are you going to do to improve them?

6. Proverbs 29:18 says, "Where there is no vision the people perish." If vision requires a God inspiration for birthing the vision, activities to test the vision, and your sacrifice to make the vision a reality, do you have a Godly vision that needs to be pursued? What is it and what do you think are the next steps to pursue it? If you have no such vision, is this something you have been or should be considering?

7. A critical reason vision is important is that it provides hope. Hope is the sense or confidence that something can be attained. Are you a hopeful person? Do you provide hope for those you lead whether it's your family, church, or business associates?

8. Take a few minutes and meditate on humility. How do you view humility? As a strength or a weakness? Is this something you truly possesses or would like to possess?

9. Write out your definition of what it means to be a servant. Give examples of people you know who serve well or have a servant's heart. What sets them apart?

10. Think about an encounter with an individual that you know will happen this week. Now think about this encounter as an opportunity to serve sacrificially. What does that level of intentionality look like? Commit to follow through on this opportunity this week.

11. How have you seen the impact of mentorship in your own life? Write a specific story and tell of the impact it has had. (If you haven't, what is your plan to get a mentor?)

12. If you do not have an "older mentor" or "peer mentor," begin praying for God to bring someone to mind who you could pursue. Write down who this person might be and why you are seeking them out specifically. What are qualities that draw you to them? And what qualities do you want to learn from them?

13. What is one action item you want to take from this chapter?

DO Impact your World

To Honor God is the first of four principles we have been studying over the last few lessons. It is the "being" aspect of our relationship with God. Serving People is the first "doing" aspect of how we Honor God. Before we can best serve people, it is important to understand the unique gifts and talents God has given to each of us. When we understand our gifts we really begin to understand what we can become passionate about. During this Passion section of the LIFE plan, we are going to dig in and hopefully find out how God has wired you, what you get excited about, and begin to ask God for a vision as to how you can serve him with a full head, a full heart and skillful hands.

Live With Passion

This section helps you understand how God made you and what special talents, abilities, skills and desires He gave you to serve Him in the most impactful way possible. Either use the Planning Cards that come with this study or download a copy of the LIFE plan at http://go.enterprisestewardship.com/annual-plan. Keep your LIFE Plan document handy. I actually keep my planning cards or downloaded plan (folded in half) in the back of my LIFE book. Let's get started in completing your LIFE plan.

Personality Profile / Natural Giftings God has made all of us in His own image. At the same time, He made each of us unique, each with our own special abilities. Use this section to help you discover and affirm how God has wired you. Start by answering the question "What are my natural gifts?" This is an intuitive look at who you think you are. We have also found it helpful to get an outside view by asking a few close friends who know you well to comment on your strengths. Additionally, we would encourage you to take a personality assessment that will give you more self-awareness and help you discover your strengths. We recommend the Strength Finders Assessment, DISC, and Enneagram. Here is how you can access each of these tools:

Strength Finders - https://www.gallupstrengthscenter.com

DISC - https://www.discprofile.com

Enneagram - https://www.enneagraminstitute.com/

Action Item: Go the Annual Plan Passion card in the LIFE Plan. In the Personality Profile/Natural Giftings section, record what you perceive to be your natural giftings. This will come from your own thoughts as well as what other people have said about you. Log the results of any personality profile you may have taken here also.

What Excites Me? We are so often immersed in the day-to-day grind of our lives that we don't ask the simple question: What excites me? Ask it now. List three things or ideas that really light your fire. What do you think or dream about in your leisure time? Is there a problem in your community, state, nation or the world for which you have a strong burden? Your hobbies are often a great indication of your passions, so list them here also.

Action Item: On your plan, write down three or four things or ideas that really fire you up. What are three or four things you would like to do other than what you are doing right now in your life?

Skills I Possess / Life Experiences. What skills do you possess? What formal education have you had? Your experiences in life, particularly those in the jobs you have held, will tell you a great deal about your passions. What did you like in those jobs? What did you dislike? And most importantly, what are the three most valuable skills you have learned in those jobs? Which of them provides the greatest satisfaction as you do them?

Action Item: On your plan, write down your answers to the skills questions above.

IMPACT 50. Now is the time for you to think BIG and STRATEGIC. Here is the question: What should you be spending time on TODAY that will have a great impact 50 years from now? In this drive-through, hurry up, disposable world, the question seems almost absurd. But it is a most important question if you are to live with great impact.

> Starting Businesses
>
> Running companies
>
> Leading people
>
> Develop vision and executable plans
>
> Pouring into the lives of young people

Assess your gifts and talents, consider your experience, embrace what you are passionate about, and ask God to give you a vision for how your life can really make a difference. A good friend of mine ran for mayor of Midland, Texas, for the sole purpose of solving the city's major problem of having no water. It took five years and a monumental effort, but the city of Midland will now have water for the next 100 years. Great impact follows great vision. What is God calling you to do?

Action Item: Have fun with this section! Give yourself the freedom to dream big. Write down your IMPACT 50 goals. What do you believe God is calling you to take responsibility for stewarding?

PASSION
PERSONALITY PROFILE

Gallop: Achiever, Analytic, Strategist

Enneagram: 7 With Wing of 8

THREE THINGS THAT EXCITE ME.

1. Starting & Building Enterprises

2. Young People

3. Business

THREE THINGS I DO WELL.

1. Communicator

2. Strategy

3. Team Building

IMPACT 50

To transform the minds and hearts of young people by
creating a new method of education that is affordable,
experiential, and Christ centered.

SUMMARY

Continue to think through your passions and how you are having or can have an impact on those around you. Don't be afraid to embrace your natural abilities and align those with things you believe God is calling you to do.

Be daring and audacious with your vision for your Impact 50 goals. How can you make those things a reality in your life?

Read: Pride and Humility, Thomas A. Tarrants, III, D.Min http://www.cslewisinstitute.org/ webfm_send/890

Watch: What makes a good life? Lessons from the Longest Study on Happiness, Robert Waldinger, https://www.youtube.com/ watch?v=8KkKuTCFvzI&feature=youtu.be

Excellence is to do a common thing in an uncommon way.

Booker T. Washington

Lesson 5

LIFE Plan - Platform Character & Connection

KNOW

This week you will be challenged to live with excellence.

BELIEVE

You will learn the what, why, and how of three key virtues to becoming excellent: expertise, innovation, and discipline.

DO

We will begin to complete the Platform section of the personal plan dealing with Character and Connection.

EXPERTISE INNOVATION

PURSUE
EXCELLENCE

DISCIPLINE

KNOW Invest in Yourself

Excellence is a powerful principle because it allows you to Honor God and inspire your fellow man. Excellence is doing the best you can, where you are, with what you have, for the glory of God. The difference between excellence and arrogance is motivation. Are you doing it to glorify you or to glorify God? God's word is the final authority on becoming excellent in our relationship with Jesus and our relationships with our fellow man. Excellence is also commanded; it is not an optional part of the Christian life. Excellence is a result of pursuing with great vigor expertise, innovation, and discipline.

Here are your assignments for this lesson.

Memorize Colossians 3:23

> Whatever you do, work at it with all your heart, as working for the Lord, not for human masters.

Read Chapter 5 in *A High Impact LIFE*. Highlight the concepts that spoke deeply to you. Be prepared to discuss these highlights with your small group.

Watch: Why Do We Pursue Excellence? Austin Stone Worship, https://www.youtube.com/watch?time_continue=9&v=QiqUKbUkJYY

Read: Lessons on Leadership Excellence from Paul, Brent Crowe, https://factsandtrends. net/2018/09/12/2-lessons-on-leadership- excellence-from-paul/

BELIEVE ♡ Be Inspired

In the last lesson we were challenged to honor God through service to your fellow man. In this lesson, we will reflect on how we pursue excellence. I think many of us know the power of excellence but aren't willing to make the effort and exert the discipline to make it a reality.

If we are going to be excellent, we have to believe that it is really an important part of our Christian walk. Colossians 3:23 tells us that "whatever ever we do, do it as working for the Lord and not for ourselves." If we are doing it for the Lord, we must do it to the best of our abilities. As you work through the following exercises, I would challenge you to step up your game and strive to be better- not to glorify the created, but to glorify the Creator.

1. Connection gets you in the game. In other words, it's often your relationships in life that open doors for you. But its Competence that keeps you in the game. If you were to take an honest assessment of your competence in whatever platform (business, education, ministry, homemaker, spouse, parent) God has placed you, would you be happy with the results? If you are not satisfied, where do you need to improve?

2. Serving people requires leadership. Pursuing excellence

requires managing. Do your natural gifts lean more toward leadership or management? What are you going to do to ensure you live with excellence in both of these areas?

3. We must not confuse excellence (honoring God) with arrogance (honoring me). Can you truly say you are an excellent versus an arrogant person? In what areas do you tend towards arrogance? Provide a brief commentary on excellence versus arrogance as it pertains to how we live as Christians.

4. If the three virtues to achieving excellence are expertise, innovation, and discipline, which one(s) of those come naturally to you? If there is one that does not come naturally, is this important to work on and if so, what are you going to do about it?

5. If expertise is broadly defined as spending 10,000 hours on a particular subject, do you consider yourself an "expert" in any given thing? If yes, what is it and how can you use this gift to further glorify God? If you don't consider yourself an expert, what could you be an expert in based on your natural giftings and what are the steps you should take to begin that journey?

6. Innovation sets our actions apart. It makes a difference in the impact we have. Review your current platform in life. What are three innovative things you could do in this role that would greatly leverage your impact?

7. Do you attach positive or negative connotations to the word "discipline?" What area of your life do you need to exert more discipline? What will you do to ensure you are accountable in being a more disciplined person?

8. Three important tools to becoming a disciplined person are the annual LIFE Plan, accountability, and understanding your rhythm of life. Reread the section on "Practicing a Disciplined Life"

(last pages of Chapter 5) in High Impact LIFE. Reflect on these tools and determine if you truly view them as important in helping you become a more disciplined person. Journal your reflections.

9. The discipline of spending quality time with God on a daily basis is essential. Reflect and journal your thoughts on how you exercise this discipline. Include the specifics of time in God's word, time in fervent prayer, time in meditation on and memorization of God's word.

10. The discipline of developing great relationships will result in great impact not only on others but on yourself. Reflect on this discipline and journal your thoughts including the types of people you spend time with, the quantity and quality of these relationships, and your thoughts with how you could improve your connectability.

11. Identify an individual, family, church, or business that you believe represents excellence in all they do with the sole purpose of glorifying God. Write down all of the things they do to create excellence. Can you apply or adopt any of these attributes to your own life?

DO ✋ Impact your World

In our first lesson together you learned how to create a weekly strategy and in our second lesson the importance of daily execution. Lesson 3 commenced the creation of your LIFE plan by focusing on PURPOSE, and you added PASSION in Lesson 4. Hopefully by now you have a good sense of your purpose, what gifts and talents you have been given, and the start of a long-term vision for how your LIFE can impact the world.

ACTION ITEM: How are you doing on your weekly strategy? Are you completing it? Are you looking at it every morning before you start your day? Are you reviewing it at the end of the day to see how you are doing? How is your daily execution working? Are you establishing a rhythm to your day by doing the important things first?

LIFE PLAN

In this lesson we are going to focus on the third section of your LIFE plan: your PLATFORM. This section is where you will begin to take your dreams and aspirations and turn them into measurable goals and specific action items that will literally change your life. Take a minute and locate the LIFE plan template. You should either have a set of the LIFE Plan cards or you can download a copy of the plan at http://go.enterprisestewardship.com/annual-plan of check out page 94 in the back of the book.

By now you should have completed the Purpose and Passion sections of your plan. Go to the PLATFORM section and you will see that it is divided into four sections. These sections represent the four key areas in your LIFE. If you are pursuing excellence in these four basic areas, you will be well on your way to living with great impact. Here are the four areas and aspects of your life that will be impacted:

1. **Character** – Honor God in all you do. This section is meant to help you grow in your spiritual life. It will challenge you to set goals that will increase your personal time with God, to exercise more faith, and to live more obediently according to God's word.

2. **Connection** – Serve People in extraordinary ways. This section will challenge you to set goals to increase your personal connection and influence with those you know and love.

You will set goals for your family, your involvement in the Christian community, and be challenged to grow your influence at work.

3. **Competence** – Pursue excellence in all you do. In this section you will be challenged to become excellent in your mental and emotional well being, your vocational expertise, and your physical health.

4. **Commitment** – Steward the many resources God has given you to manage. You will set goals to make sure you are spending your time and money wisely. And you will be challenged to prayerfully consider how God wants to use you to live with great impact by thinking through your Impact 50 vision.

Life Assessment

Before we get into creating goals and action items to help you improve in these four key areas, it's important to understand where you currently are. Included in the life plan template is a tool called your LIFE ASSESSMENT. This is a tool that will allow you to assess your LIFE in four major categories: Character, Connection, Competence, and Commitment. To use this tool, go to the assessment section of your plan and score yourself in the 12 specific categories. Answer each question and rate yourself 0 to 5, 0 meaning you need much work in this category and 5 meaning you are doing it very well. Once you have answered the questions, go to the wheel of Life and plot your answers. For example, if you gave yourself a 3 in Competence/Physical, then color in the 1-3 blocks in the circle. Once you have colored in all of the blocks you will have a very good sense graphically of where you need to concentrate to have a well-rounded and balanced LIFE. Imagine your life represents a wheel rolling through LIFE. If you have a wheel out of balance, your journey through life will be bumpy. On the other hand, if your wheel is smooth and balanced your journey will be much more pleasant and rewarding. Work on smoothing out your wheel. Work on the low numbers, even at the expense of the high numbers so that you have a well rounded LIFE wheel.

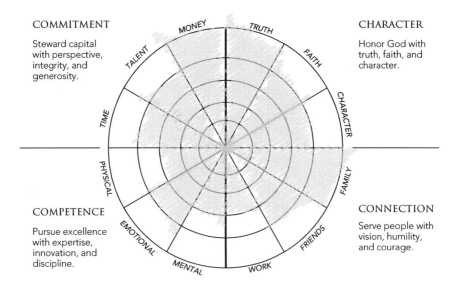

COMMITMENT

Steward capital with perspective, integrity, and generosity.

CHARACTER

Honor God with truth, faith, and character.

COMPETENCE

Pursue excellence with expertise, innovation, and discipline.

CONNECTION

Serve people with vision, humility, and courage.

PLATFORM – Character and Connection

During this lesson we will focus on your Character (your relationship with God) and Connection (your relationship with people). As you look at the Platform section of the LIFE Plan cards or worksheet, there are four columns. They are: Virtues, Goals, Action Items, and Status. Let's take a look at each.

Virtues: Along the left-hand side of the page (printed vertically) are the major areas of your life that need your attention. When you are functioning at some level of competence and commitment in all of these key areas, your LIFE will be in balance and you will feel much greater satisfaction and contentment in LIFE. You will be living a High Impact LIFE.

Goals: Please list one to three goals that you would like to accomplish for the specific virtue noted to the left of this column. These goals will often be related to how you assessed your LIFE in the LIFE assessment exercise. For areas where you are low you will need to set goals that will help you become better in each category.

Action Item: If you are to attain your Goal, you will need to define an action item or two that will help you achieve this goal. Define an action that will accomplish the goal in the column to the left. This action item should be specific, time sensitive, and measurable.

Status Q1 through Q4: Each quarter you should assess your position to see if you are achieving your goals. Log these assessments in the four columns (one per calendar quarter) at the far right-hand side of the page. This quarterly assessment should be completed with your running buddy to allow for maximum accountability. When assessing your progress, you will use one of three indicators to assess your current state of progress. If you have failed at your action item, put a (-) in the box. If you made an attempt but it was not done with excellence, then put a (0). If you completed the Action Item with excellence, give yourself a (+). Make sure that you and your running buddy are in agreement as to your assessment.

Character: This is the upward spiritual/morale capacity (quotient) that drives our convictions (passion) through Faith to Honor God. In this section you should reflect on three key areas that affect your character in your life: truth, faith, and character (choices). Think about where you would like to be in each of these areas and then determine actionable items you can pursue to help you improve in each of these areas. Though these areas will affect you mostly inwardly, they will affect how the outward facing choices you make as you interact with people at home and at work. Think about daily choices you can make to improve each of these areas.

Connection: The outward Emotional/Relational capacity (quotient) that drives our Compassion (vision) through Love to Serve People. In this section you should reflect on three key relationships you foster: family, friends, and work. Think about how you serve these people. Do you serve them with vision, humility, and courage? Prayerfully consider how God may be prompting you to grow in these relationships. Are there some relationships that are being prioritized above another area? Think about how you can evaluate how your time and attention are being spent.

SUMMARY

1. Are you completing your weekly strategy worksheets?

2. Are you executing daily?

3. Have you completed the personal assessment?

4. Have you found a running buddy?

5. Have you completed the character and connection sections of the life plan?

One last comment related to your LIFE Plan. If your purpose in life is to honor God and enjoy Him forever, two critical aspects of your spiritual life must be in balance: abiding and doing. These are abiding and doing (John 15). Or you might say trusting and obeying (John 14). Or faith and work (James 2). If your Personal Plan becomes a tool that allows you to please God only by your works, it will be a legalistic tool to measure your love for God only by your "doing." Such a plan is destined for failure. Instead, focus your plan on "abiding" in Christ. That is why the character section emphasizes time in God's word, prayer, meditation, worship, and fellowship. If we truly abide, we can ultimately do – not for our glory, but His.

We make a living by what we get, but we make a life by what we give.

Winston Churchill

Lesson 6
LIFE Plan - Platform - Competence & Commitment

KNOW

We will delve into one of the most impactful concepts to living a High Impact LIFE: stewardship, the trusted management of another's possession.

BELIEVE

Stewardship takes the most amount of faith because you are handing over to God all that you are, all that you have, and all that you might become.

DO

During this lesson you will complete your personal plan by setting goals and action items in the areas of Competence and Commitment.

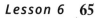

Invest in Yourself

This week we will be discussing the importance of stewardship. Stewardship is the careful management of something entrusted to ones' care. Stewardship demands that we give thoughtful attention to the owner's intents and wishes for his property and resources. Stewardship is a transformational mindset that will allow us to live open handedly. As we pivot from the mindset of ownership to stewardship, the freedom, joy, and expectation for God to work mightily in our lives will bring us more satisfaction and contentment than we can imagine.

We live in a world completely contradictory to this concept of stewardship. It's a world that teaches us to get all that you can get. The key to living a life of stewardship goes back to our very first lesson together. Are we living for ourselves or for something greater than ourselves? Are we pursuing success or living surrendered?

Here are your assignments for this lesson.

Memorize Luke 16:11

> So if you have not been trustworthy in handling worldly wealth, who will trust you with true riches?

Read Chapter 6 in *A High Impact LIFE*. Highlight the concepts that spoke deeply to you. Be prepared to discuss these highlights with your small group.

Read: Should Christians Seek Wealth Creation?, Dr. Anne Bradley, https://tifwe.org/should-christians-seek-wealth-creation/

Read: How Are You Investing Your Life? CBMC, https://www.cbmcint.com/how-are-you-investing-your-life/

BELIEVE  Be Inspired

In the last lesson we reflected on how we pursue excellence. In this lesson, we will focus on how we steward the various resources in our life.

Stewardship is a powerful paradigm that will radically change the way you live if you will embrace the fact that it will challenge your faith walk on a daily basis. A life of stewardship is not for the faint hearted or weak-kneed. The primary character trait required to be a steward is Commitment. A commitment to understand through Perspective that God owns it all and then a commitment to exercise integrity to actually live it out. The result is a LIFE of generosity.

Think & Reflect

1. Stewardship is the careful management of something entrusted to our care. It demands that we give thoughtful attention to the owners' intents and wishes for their property and capital. Based on this definition, what areas of your life do you steward

well? What areas of your life need improvement?

2. Based on the section on Leadership versus Management, do you consider yourself a leader or a manager? If a steward is one who artfully brings these two disciplines together into a powerful unified approach, what are two or three things you can do now to improve the weaker of these to areas? Who will hold you accountable to improve in this area?

3. Perspective by definition is the ability to view things related to their true importance to everything else. How would you define your perspective on life, and in particular your perspective on stewardship? Is it a nice idea or a foundational principle that you live out on a daily basis?

4. Ownership is important to us but stewardship is important to God. Consequently we need to know His perspective so we can manage His assets in a way that is pleasing to Him. Reflect on your knowledge of God. Do you really know Him and His amazing attributes? What are you going to do to know God better?

5. Knowing God is essential; living by faith is required. Does your life reflect a life of stewardship? Does it reflect a life of deep daily faith by how you live? How can you begin to live differently so that you can bear witness to a suspicious, unbelieving world that you are a God-fearing, people-loving, excellence-pursuing follower of Jesus?

6. Perspective is a head thing. Most of us will easily acknowledge that God owns it all. But exercising integrity is often a different thing. It is a heart thing, a deep belief in what you know to be true. Our faith is oftentimes the biggest impediment in living a life of stewardship. Reflect on your life as a faithful steward. In what areas do you demonstrate great faith? What areas do you need to exercise greater faith?

7. Living as a steward is an outward demonstration of our inward faith. It is how we show the world that Christ has transformed out hearts and impacted our lives. The end game is radical generosity. It's how we love our neighbor as we love ourselves. Reflect on your life as it pertains to generosity. Are you generous with your time? Your talent? And your treasure? Are you radically generous (requiring great faith) or are you comfortable in your generosity, giving only out of your excess?

8. True generosity is done with the sole motivation to bless another regardless of the benefits that may accrue to the giver. Reflect on your motivation for being generous. Is your generosity driven by duty and obligation or your desire to be a good and faithful steward? How do we change our motivations in life?

9. Do you think of generosity as a giving thing or a living thing? In other words, is it one of the many spiritual disciplines you check off a list or is it an all-encompassing approach to LIFE?

10. Please reflect and respond to four critical habits of generosity below.

    a. Generosity takes faith. Are you exercising faith in your generosity?

    b. Generosity needs a plan. Do you have a plan? If no, sit down with your spouse and devise a giving plan for the next year.

    c. Generosity requires accountability. What does this look like for you?

    d. Generosity requires asking hard questions. Are you asking the hard questions?

11. Too often we convince ourselves that generosity is not about the amount but the attitude of the heart. Matthew 6:21 tells us that for where our treasure is, so there is our heart. In other words, the amount counts, because it is an indication of our heart.

Does your generosity cost you something? Does is cause you to take some risk with your time, talent, and treasure? Does it crimp your lifestyle?

12. Of the three areas where we can demonstrate generosity (time, talent, and treasure), which area is the most difficult for you to be generous? Which is the easiest? Over the next week look to see how you can demonstrate generosity in your weak area. This will take courage and probably lots of faith. What step of faith this week will you take to be generous?

13. Are you open minded, open hearted, and open handed in your generosity?

14. Are you generous in telling others about the life-giving power of a relationship with Jesus Christ? Have you been stingy in sharing the good news with your fellow man?

DO ✋ Impact your World

Let's do a quick review of the three High Impact Habits.

1. **Weekly Strategy Sheet.** By now you should have completed five weeks of a weekly strategy sheet. If you are not completing this weekly exercise do not give up. Stay with it. It will pay great dividends if you stay with it.

2. **Daily Execution.** Have you established your rhythm for the day? Are you spending time with God and spending time reviewing and planning your day?

3. **LIFE plan.** During the last three lessons, we have been

working on your LIFE Plan: your Purpose, your Passions, and your Character and Commitment in the Platform section. If you have not completed these sections of the plan, go back now and do your best to complete the plan to the best of your ability.

PLATFORM – Competence and Commitment

During this lesson we will complete your personal plan. Today you will complete the Competence and Commitment areas in the Platform section.

Competence. In this section you should reflect on three key areas that affect your ability to live an Excellent LIFE: your emotional, mental, and physical well being. Think about where you would like to be in each of these areas and then determine actionable items you pursue to help you improve in each of these areas. These areas will affect your family life, your work, your church, and the community in which you live. These may include goals that will improve your career, make you an expert, challenge you to be innovative, and certainly improve your discipline.

Commitment. This section will focus on the stewardship of your time, talent, and treasure. Prayerfully consider what God might have you do in each of these areas. Are there areas where you should spend more resources or are there some areas that need to be trimmed back to allow for more balance in your LIFE?

SUMMARY

Continue to develop your Platform. How are you Honoring God and developing your character? How are you Serving People and connecting with them? How are you Pursuing Excellence and honing your competence? How are you Stewarding Resources and expanding your commitment?

Watch: Biblical Stewardship and Business, Stephen Grabil, https://www.youtube.com/watch?v=D43ixsQfNh4

Read: The Healing Power of Economics, Jeff Haanen, https://denverinstitute.org/healing-power-economics-christianity-today-book-review/

PLATFORM

CHARACTER | HONOR GOD

	GOALS	ACTION ITEMS	Q1	Q2	Q3	Q4
TRUTH	1. DAILY TIME IN GOD'S WORD. 2. REVIEW THIS VERSE DAILY.	MEMORIZE BIBLE RESPOND PLAN. WEEKLY REVIEW WITH RUNNING BUDDY.				
FAITH	1. DAILY TIME IN GOD'S WORD. 2. REVIEW THIS VERSE DAILY.	MEMORIZE BIBLE RESPOND PLAN. WEEKLY REVIEW WITH RUNNING BUDDY.				
CHARACTER	WALK THE TALK.	WEEKLY MENTORING WITH RUNNING BUDDY.				

CONNECTION | SERVE PEOPLE

	GOALS	ACTION ITEMS	Q1	Q2	Q3	Q4
FAMILY	1. HONOR MY WIFE. 2. TIME W/KIDS	MONTHLY DATE W/WIFE WEEKEND ACTIVITIES W/KIDS				
FRIENDS	DEVELOP FRIENDSHIP W/NEW COUPLES.	MONTHLY DINNER AT HOUSE				
WORK	BECOME MORE VISIBLE TO PEOPLE I LEAD	WEEKLY PLANT TOUR.				

COMPETENCE | PURSUE EXCELLENCE

	GOALS	ACTION ITEMS	Q1	Q2	Q3	Q4
MENTAL	2 BOOKS/MONTH	DEVELOP READING LIST OUTLINE EACH BOOK AS READ.				
EMOTIONAL	DECLUTTER MIND	NO SCREENS AFTER 6 § SUNDAY				
PHYSICAL	200 LBS DAILY WORKOUT	1,800 CALORIES/DAILY 100 PUSH UPS, 100 SIT UPS				

COMMITMENT | STEWARD RESOURCES

	GOALS	ACTION ITEMS	Q1	Q2	Q3	Q4
TIME	KNOW MY G-KIDS	WEEKLY SCHOOL LUNCH. WEEKEND PROJECT - TREEHOUSE				
TALENT	DEEP DIVE INTO FAITH § WORK	WEEKLY READS OUTLINE BUSINESS PHILOSOPHY				
MONEY	DESIGN ANNUAL GIVING PLAN	1.WRITE PLAN W/SPOUSE 2.ATTEND GIVING CONFERENCE				

Capital is wealth we are willing to invest, to put at risk with the expectation of a greater reward.

Pete Ochs

Lesson 7

Personal Financial Plan

KNOW

In this lesson we will learn to flourish as we create economic, social, and spiritual capital.

BELIEVE

Prayerfully think through your platform and then exercise great faith by stepping out and earnestly serving the Lord in great obedience.

DO

You will complete a personal financial statement showing your assets, liabilities, and net worth along with completing a personal budget for your income and expenses.

KNOW ◯ Invest in Yourself

Flourishing requires the creation of economic, social, and spiritual wealth. For those of us who have chosen to live as stewards instead of owners, our primary challenge will be to always reinvest our excess wealth- our economic, social and spiritual capital- back into projects and people to further God's kingdom here on earth. Will we hoard our excess wealth, or will we put it to work?

During this lesson we will visit the concept of flourishing. How can you be all that God wants you to be- particularly in light of how He has gifted you? We will tackle the three key components needed for you to flourish:

1. Sufficient material provision.
2. Deep authentic relationships.
3. An eternal Purpose for living.

Once we understand these basic requirements for flourishing, we will delve into how these can be made manifest in the platform God has given you.

Here are your assignments for this lesson.

Memorize John 15:5

> I am the vine; you are the branches. If you remain in me and I in you, you will bear much fruit; apart from me you can do nothing.

Read Chapter 7 in *A High Impact LIFE*. Highlight the concepts that spoke deeply to you. Be prepared to discuss these highlights with your small group.

Read: Asking Tough Questions about the
Provision and Purpose of Government, Dr. Paul
Cleveland, https://tifwe.org/what-is-the-purpose-
of-government/

Watch: Commissioned to Flourish, Andy
Crouch, https://www.youtube.com/
watch?v=Zgl5DaZKmD4

BELIEVE ♡ Be Inspired

In the last lesson, we focused on how we steward the various
resources in our life. In this lesson, we will explore living a LIFE
of flourishing, which requires great faith. It requires an ability to
understand that your life needs to include material provision, great
relationships, and a purpose for living. The tendency for most of
us is to focus on material provision either out of fear or greed. Our
relationship with others and with God often get short changed
because of our focus on financial gain and security. Please read and
reflect on the following questions which will hopefully lead you to
a life of living by faith every day.

1. As you reflect on the amount of energy and effort you
pursue in living a LIFE of flourishing- that is pursuing economic
capital, social capital, and spiritual capital- would you consider your
life to be well-balanced? If not, where are you struggling to achieve

balance?

2. If poverty is not enough and wealth is enough, do you consider yourself to be wealthy in all three areas of flourishing: economically, socially, and spiritually?

3. If wealth is enough and capital is more than enough, which one or more of the three forms of wealth (economic, social, or spiritual) would you say that you have more than enough?

4. If capital is excess wealth we are willing to put at risk with the expectation of a greater reward, are you risking whatever talents God has given you? Are you investing your financial resources (economic capital), your time (social capital), and faith, (spiritual capital) into your family, friends, and community?   If not, why? If not, have you included making this a change in your life by including it as a goal on your LIFE Plan?

5. Read the parable of the talents in Matthew 25. What talents has God given you?   Are you investing your talents by putting them to work or are you hoarding your talents by "burying them in the bottom of your tent"?   What changes will you make in your life to ensure that you are not hoarding your talents?

6. Examine your personal financial statement and personal budget. Have you set a finish line for when you will cease to accumulate financial wealth? How much is enough both from a net worth perspective and a standard of living perspective?

7. Genesis 2:15 tells us God put man in the garden to work. Do you enjoy the work you do? Is it satisfying and fulfilling? Do you view work as sacred or secular?

8. Read Ecclesiastes 3:22.   Do you view the challenges you face daily in your work as a burden or a way to rely on God for his faithfulness and strength? If challenges are a burden, how will you

work to change that attitude?

9. If social capital is the mutual benefits derived by a group of like-minded people pursuing a common cause, what group(s) of people are you associated with and what is your common cause?

10. If you were to reflect on the social capital that is being created in your immediate family, where would you rank it on a scale from 1 to 10 with 10 being the best? What are the main things that deter your family from being a place where relationships are always great? What are you going to do to fix these detrimental things that affect your family relationships?

11. How involved are you in your local community or neighborhood? Are you a taker or a giver when it comes to social capital in your community? How much time do you spend volunteering to make your community a better place to live? Are you an instrument of flourishing in your community?

12. If Spiritual Capital is the Purpose you have in LIFE, have you really defined your Purpose? Do you REALLY believe that Jesus is who He says he is and do you live like it? Would the people closest to you agree with your previous answer?

13. As a country, why do we struggle to come together over the many things that divide us? What are you going to do to make a difference in the lives of the people you live with?

14. Do you believe that Spiritual capital is more important than economic or social capita? If so, why? If not, why not?

15. If the essence of spiritual capital is to Honor God, comment on your pursuit of Truth, your willingness to live by Faith, and your obedience to live with Character. Have you taken into account your current status and the changes you would like to make in each of these as you completed your LIFE Plan?

16. What is your current platform (job, family, social,

influence)? Define your platform. Take some time to dream of ways God might create economic, social, and spiritual capital through your platform. Be creative. God is not limited. What steps do you need to take to maximize your capital?

DO ✋ Impact your World

Weekly Strategy. Are you spending 30 minutes one time per week laying out the strategy that will allow you to do the important instead of the urgent?

MEMORY VERSES   ENTERPRISE STEWARDSHIP LIFE PLAN

1 JOHN 2:15-16 | WHY
Do not love the world or anything in the world. If anyone loves the world, the Father is not in them. For everything in the world—the lust... the pride of life—comes not...

GA
I hav
bod

MA
Jesu
mind

MA
For e
for m

COL
What

LUKE
So if y

JOHN
"I am t
apart fr

2 CO
Therefo

P U
PERSC

To ke
husb
entre

PERSON

Honor
Serve F
Pursue
Stewar

Weekly Strategy ——— COURAGE ——— Date ———

Daily Repeatable Activities	Sunday
TIME W/GOD	CHURCH
AFFIRM SPOUSE	REVIEW ANNUAL PLAN WEEKLY STRATEGY

Monday	Tuesday
CONFERENCE CALL ON BUDGET LETTER TO LEGISLATORS	FINE TUNE CONF. PLAN FOLLOW UP W/JANE — PLAN SESSION RUNNING BUDDY

Wednesday	Thursday
LEADERSHIP TRAINING FOLLOW-UP PHONE CALLS	MENTOR MTG

Friday	Saturday
DEVELOP OVERVIEW OF COMPANY PRESENTATION CIRCULATE TO KEY LEADERSHIP TEAM	FAMILY DAY DINNER WITH KIDS

ENTERPRISE STEWARDSHI LIFE PLA

To Do List
← Revisions for company plan
○ Review Annual Plan
  Coordinate with team on budget revisions
  Where do we have room to develop leadership
  training? What are other organizations toing
  in this space.
  Coordinate with managers on Teams
← Latest on Book Revisions

people by
ffordable,

Daily Execution. Have you developed your daily rhythm and are you taking time at the beginning of the day to really get to know God, and then plan out the rest of your day?

LIFE Plan. Have you completed your LIFE Plan?

During this lesson you will complete both a personal financial statement and an annual budget.

Personal Financial Statement. This is simply a snapshot of where you are financially with regards to what you own (your assets) and what you owe (your liabilities). The difference between these two is your net worth. Hopefully this number is positive. If it is negative, you would be considered bankrupt because what you owe (your liabilities) are greater than what you own (your assets). Download the forms at http://go.enterprisestewardship.com/annual-plan.

This form is very simple to complete. List all of your assets and all of your debts. The difference will be your net worth. Save this form and over the years you will be amazed at how your net worth will grow. Remember, "Steady plodding brings prosperity, hasty speculation brings poverty."

Annual Budget. The personal financial statement is a measure of what you own and owe. The Annual Budget shows how much income you make and how much money you spend over the course of a year. If you are spending more than you make, it will not take long and you will become bankrupt (liabilities greater than your assets) because you will more than likely be borrowing money from the bank or on credit cards to subsidize your lifestyle. Here are several key principles that you need to ensure are happening as you complete your annual budget:

1. You must take this exercise seriously and be absolutely honest and accurate regarding all of your income and expenses.

2. Your income must exceed your expenses. If it doesn't, then you must reduce your expenses to less than your income and it must happen NOW.

3. Included in your expenses should be two very important expense line items:

a. **Giving.** Make sure you are a generous person. The target for this amount needs to be at least 10% of your income. This is often difficult to do. It comes down to this question, do you really believe that "he who sows generously will reap generously?" Giving takes faith, but it is commanded and the benefits you will experience will be out of this world.

b. **Saving.** Make sure that you are putting money away for long term savings and investment. This would be for retirement. This amount should be 10% of your income. If it can't be right now, then over the next three years you should make this a goal to save 10% of your income. Here is why this is important. The average American family that makes $60,000 per year. If a family saves $6,000 per year, at a very conservative investment yielding 7% annually, after 40 years of work the value of your retirement will be $1.2 million! If you continue to earn 7% this will allow you to earn $84,000 per year and never touch the $1.2 million.

SUMMARY

What vocation, career, and job has God called you to and are

ENTERPRISE STEWARDSHIP
LIFE PLAN

PERSONAL BUDGET

Personal Balance Sheet

INCOME	BUDGET	ACTUAL
Salary, Bonuses, Commissions	85000	
Interest & Dividends	200	
Net Business Income	0	
Other	3800	
TOTAL INCOME	93000	

EXPENSES	EXPENSES	ACTUAL
Contributions	8500	
Gifts/Payments to Others/Alimony/Etc	1200	
Savings Short Term	2500	
Savings Long Term	6000	
Food	10000	
Clothing	6000	
Income Taxes - Fed & State	16400	
Auto Payments	4800	
Auto Maintenance	3200	
Housing - Loan Pmts or Rent	9600	
Utilites	6600	
Housing Maintenance	4400	
Real Estate Taxes	4200	
Education- Tuition/ Student Loans	7500	
TOTAL EXPENSES	90,900	
NET CASH FLOW	2100	

FINANCES

Personal Financial Statement

Assets

Cash on hand/checking account	5300
Savings/Money Market	22500
Stocks/Bonds/Mutual Funds	93000
Cash Value of Life Insurance	0
Coins & Jewelry	0
Home	235000
Other Real Estate	23000
Mortgages/Note Receivable	0
Business Valuation	0
Automobiles/Other Vehicles	$43,000
Furniture/Other Personal Property	$21,000
IRA/401(K)/Retirement	$114200
Other Assets	0
Total Assets:	557000

Debts

Credit Card Debt	500
Auto Loans	17400
Home Mortgage	168000
Medical/Other Past Due Bills	0
Other Real Estate Mortgages	16000
Bank Loans	0
Student Loans	0
Personal Debts to Family/Friends	0
Business Loans	0
Life Insurance Loans	0
Total Debts:	$201900

Total Assets	557000
Minus Total Debt	201900
Net Worth	355100

you leveraging it in a way that is pleasing and honoring to Him? Are you utilizing your finances and talents to the best of your abilities? God not only cares about what you do, but also cares How you do it. How we work has the potential to create economic, social and spiritual capital in your own life and the in the lives of others.

Read: Discovering Your True Business, Mark D. Roberts, https://www.patheos.com/blogs/markdroberts/2017/12/27/ discovering-true-business/

Efforts and courage are not enough without purpose and direction.

John F. Kennedy

Lesson 8

Personal Challenge

KNOW

What then is the purpose in striving to live a High Impact LIFE? It is to Glorify God and enjoy Him forever.

BELIEVE

Living a LIFE of impact begins with the pursuit of Truth. But it very quickly becomes a LIFE driven by faith. Faith is the fuel that turns knowing into doing.

DO

Doing is simply a matter of knowing the Truth with your head and living it out through your faith. It is a LIFE of obedience to God's Word and a trusted following of the Holy Spirit. Many know, some believe, few do.

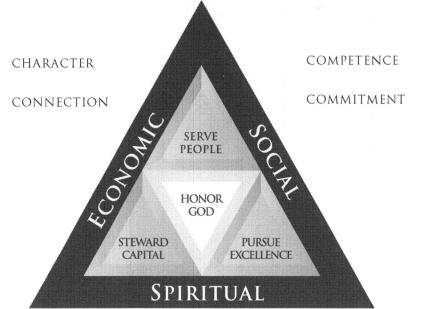

KNOW ⬤ Invest in Yourself

Congratulations on finishing a plan that will lead you to the start of a High Impact LIFE. This is not an easy journey and will often lead to great challenges and sacrifice. But it will be fulfilling beyond our imagination, particularly if we are greeted by the Father with the words, "Well done, good and faithful servant."

Our time together thus far has been spent understanding the key points to living a High Impact LIFE. This is a LIFE that starts with us unequivocal understanding that our Purpose in LIFE is to Honor God. When we truly understand our Purpose, our Passions become transformed. Our old self which sought pride, pleasure, and possessions is now redeemed to a new self, a self-desiring to Serve People, Pursue Excellence, and Steward Capital. This results in our desire to live for something greater than ourselves with the result being a Platform, our vocational calling, which becomes a powerful tool in the hands of Almighty God.

Here are your assignments for this lesson.

Memorize 2 Corinthians: 5:17

> Therefore, if anyone is in Christ, the new creation has come: The old has gone, the new is here!

Read Chapter 8 in *A High Impact LIFE*. Highlight the concepts that spoke deeply to you. Be prepared to discuss these highlights with your small group.

Read: The Disciplined Pursuit of Less, Greg McKeown, https://hbr.org/2012/08/the-disciplined-pursuit-of-less

Watch: Thomas Ellsworth: To Take Ground Where Few Dare to Stand https://www.youtube.com/watch?v=74nHFiZaA8A

BELIEVE ♡ Be Inspired

In the last lesson, we focused on living a LIFE of flourishing with great faith. This final lesson is about incorporating what we have learned into practice so we can lead a life of high impact. Do you really believe that you can make a difference? Don't just keep reading but go back and honestly answer that question. Do you really believe you can make a difference? If you don't, then ask God to burn this fact into your very soul that "if anyone is in Christ he is a new creation, the old is gone, the new has come."

You are a new person with the indwelling power of the Creator of the Universe residing in your soul ready to help you live with great impact. But you must turn the wheel of control over to Him. This requires faith that most of us don't think we can exercise. But start slow. Start with the small things where you can begin to gradually give up control and let Him operate. Just do it!

1. Are you beginning to view your life as a holistic endeavor to honor God, serve people, pursue excellence, and steward capital? Which of these areas needs additional work before you become well-balanced in these four key areas of LIFE? What are you going to do about it?

2. Based on the definitions in the book, are you flourishing? If not, what is missing?

3. Go to page 203 in the book and reread Anne Bradley's definition of flourishing. Does this look like the world in which you live? Are your family, church, neighborhood, and business community working in concert to achieve some degree of flourishing? Are you taking a leadership role in making that happen? If not, should you?

4. Living a High impact LIFE results in two distinct outcomes: a pursuit to create flourishing and "bearing fruit." Bearing fruit is the result of us "loving God with our heart, mind, soul, and loving our neighbor as ourself." Are you bearing fruit? What is holding you back?

5. Joe White with Kanakuk Kamps has a philosophy of LIFE that says, "God first, others second, I am third." Are you living a "I am third" lifestyle? What are the things keeping you from being fully engaged in this?

6. As we wind up this lesson, please take some time to prayerfully consider and honestly answer the following questions. Instead of a simple yes or no answer, think through where you do well and not so well on each question, critiquing what you can do to improve in each area.

    a. Am I loving my Purpose?

    b. Do I live with Passion?

    c. Am I leveraging my Platform?

DO ✋ Impact your World

Evaluation. Your last bit of homework will be a comprehensive exam on all that you have learned and are doing because of this study. But remember, many know, some believe, few do. So, this exam is going to test how you have been DOING! For each question below, write down an answer between 1-10 that would define how well you are DOING the activity described.

BE HONEST. When you have finished, add up all your scores and record the total on the last line.

1. Are you spending time every week to complete your Weekly Strategy? _____

2. Are you spending time every day to review your Daily Execution? _____

3. Have you fully completed your Personal Plan? _____

4. Do you have a running buddy and have you met with them? _____

5. Have you completed your Personal Financial Statement? _____

6. Have you completed your Personal Annual Budget?   ———

7. Have you memorized all your memory verses?   ———

8. Are you spending time daily with God?   ———

9. Do you have an Impact 50 vision for your LIFE?   ———

10. Are you flourishing?   ———

Total   ———

Here is where you are on the journey.

    90-100 = High Impact Knower+ Believer + Doer
    80-89 =   High Impact Knower+ Believer
    70-79 = High Impact Knower
    60-69 = Making High Impact Changes
    Less than 60 = Making Changes

SUMMARY

If your purpose in life is to honor God and enjoy Him forever, two critical aspects of your spiritual life must be in balance. These are abiding and doing (John 15). Or you might say trusting and obeying (John 14). Or faith and work (James 2). If your Personal Plan becomes a tool that allows you to please God only by your works, it will be a legalistic tool to measure your love for God only by your "doing." Such a plan is destined for failure. Instead, focus your plan on "abiding" in Christ.

A reminder as you endeavor to walk this path: choose to be a person of great Character who honor's God with truth, faith and character. Strive to connect with people to serve them with vision, humility, and courage. Endeavor to be competent and pursue excellence with expertise, innovation, and discipline. Finally, commit to stewarding resources with perspective, integrity, and generosity.

Read: Redirection not Retirement, Peter Markgraaff, https://tifwe.org/redirection-not-retirement/

Read: How to Be Content But Not Complacent, Anne Bradley, https://www.thegospelcoalition.org/article/content-not-complacent/

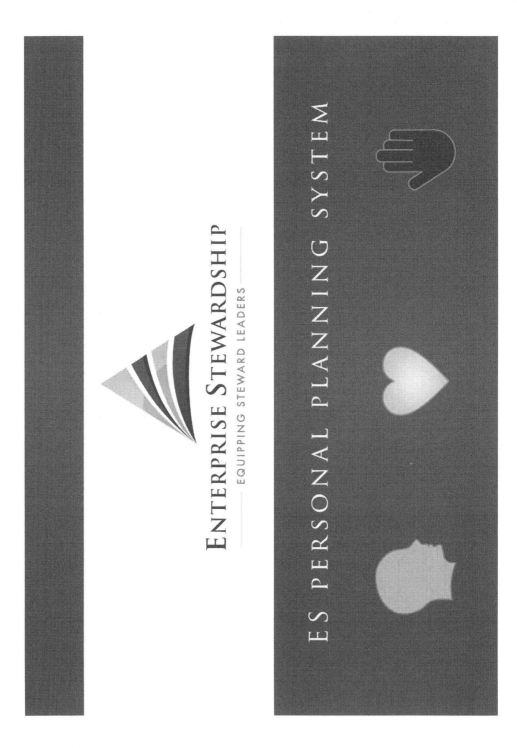

KNOW | BELIEVE | DO

PURPOSE – WHY DO I EXIST?

Vision. Spend some time prayerfully answering the question: How could I impact the world in my lifetime? During this time of deep reflection, think outside the box, dream big, and determine what the possibilities would be if there were no immovable obstacles.

PASSION – HOW DO I LIVE?

Natural giftings. God has made all of us in His own image. At the same time, He made each of us unique, each with our own special abilities. Use this section to help you figure out and affirm how God has wired you. Start by answering the question "What are my natural giftings? This is an intuitive look at who you think you are. Your friends, family, and colleagues may give you feedback on what your strengths are.

PLATFORM –WHAT AM I CALLED TO DO?

Vocation. Does my purpose in life align with what God wants it to be? Are my passions focused on allowing me to have the greatest impact for God?
Four key personality traits and their corresponding values and virtues are needed for you to leverage your platform: Character, Connection, Competence, and Commitment.

PERSONAL ASSESSMENT TOOL

Self-assess each sector of your life by giving it a value on the scale from 1 to 5, with 1 being a "state of crisis" and 5 is "flourishing." Be honest with yourself and give an accurate value which will adequately represent your satisfaction with each aspect. Graph you answers using the wheel on the back: 1 is the center, 5 is the outer ring.

CHARACTER

1. *Truth.* I consistently read, study, and memorize God's Word. ____

2. *Faith.* My prayer life is consistent, and I often will do things that require a step of faith. ____

3. *Character.* My life is in great harmony with God's expectations of how I live. ____

CONNECTION

4. *Family.* My relationships with my spouse, children, and extended family are strong and vibrant ____

5. *Friends.* I have a number of close friends who challenge and encourage me to be a better person. ____

6. *Work.* The time I spend working is in good balance with the other demands on my time. ____

COMPETENCE

7. *Mental.* I engage in activities that continually stimulate my passion for lifelong learning. ____

8. *Emotional.* I am satisfied, content, and peaceful with my position in life. ____

9. *Physical.* I eat healthy, exercise regularly, and avoid unhealthy habits. ____

COMMITMENT

10. *Time.* I am a wise steward of my time and have a good balance of work, spiritual, physical, and emotional wellbeing. ____

11. *Talent.* I consistently strive to become better in my vocational calling. ____

12. *Money.* I give, save, spend, and manage wisely the financial assets I am entrusted with. ____

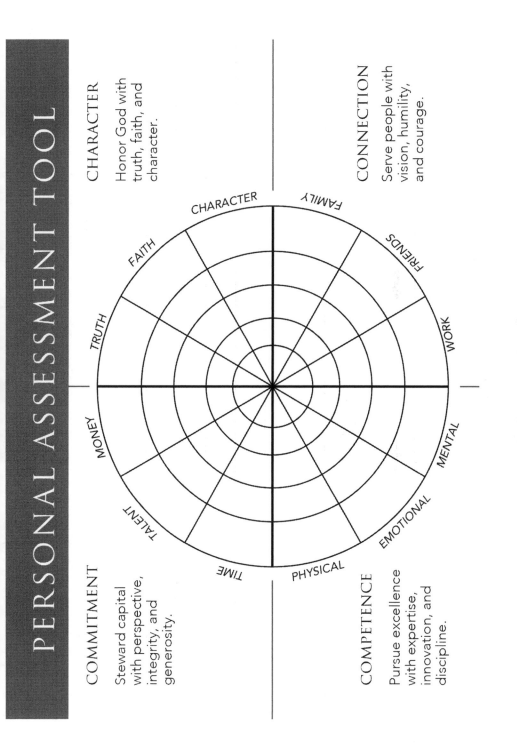

PERSONAL ASSESSMENT TOOL

CHARACTER
Honor God with truth, faith, and character.

CONNECTION
Serve people with vision, humility, and courage.

COMMITMENT
Steward capital with perspective, integrity, and generosity.

COMPETENCE
Pursue excellence with expertise, innovation, and discipline.

CHARACTER · FAITH · TRUTH · MONEY · TALENT · TIME · PHYSICAL · EMOTIONAL · MENTAL · WORK · FRIENDS · FAMILY

ANNUAL PLAN | PURPOSE

Personal Mission Statement

_____

_____

_____

_____

Personal Values

_____

_____

_____

_____

ANNUAL PLAN | MEMORY VERSES

1 JOHN 2:15-16 | WHY

Do not love the world or anything in the world. If anyone loves the world, love for the Father is not in them. For everything in the world—the lust of the flesh, the lust of the eyes, and the pride of life—comes not from the Father but from the world.

GALATIANS 2:20 | PURPOSE

I have been crucified with Christ and I no longer live, but Christ lives in me. The life I now live in the body, I live by faith in the Son of God, who loved me and gave himself for me.

MATTHEW 22:37 | HONOR GOD

Jesus replied: "Love the Lord your God with all your heart and with all your soul and with all your mind."

MARK 10:45 | SERVICE

For even the Son of Man did not come to be served, but to serve, and to give his life as a ransom for many.

COLOSSIANS 3:23 | EXCELLENCE

Whatever you do, work at it with all your heart, as working for the Lord, not for human masters.

LUKE 16:11 | STEWARDSHIP

So if you have not been trustworthy in handling worldly wealth, who will trust you with true riches?

JOHN 15:5 | FLOURISHING

I am the vine; you are the branches. If you remain in me and I in you, you will bear much fruit; apart from me you can do nothing.

2 CORINTHIANS 5:17 | TRANSFORMATION

Therefore, if anyone is in Christ, the new creation has come: The old has gone, the new is here!

ANNUAL PLAN | PASSION

THREE THINGS THAT EXCITE ME.

1.

2.

3.

THREE THINGS I DO WELL.

1.

2.

3.

ANNUAL PLAN | PASSION

PERSONALITY PROFILE

_____

_____

_____

_____

IMPACT 50

_____

_____

_____

_____

ANNUAL PLAN | PLATFORM

CHARACTER | HONOR GOD

	GOALS	ACTION ITEMS	Q1	Q2	Q3	Q4
TRUTH						
FAITH						
CHARACTER						

CONNECTION | SERVE PEOPLE

	GOALS	ACTION ITEMS	Q1	Q2	Q3	Q4
FAMILY						
FRIENDS						
WORK						

ANNUAL PLAN | PLATFORM

COMPETENCE | PURSUE EXCELLENCE

GOALS	ACTION ITEMS	Q1 Q2 Q3 Q4
MENTAL		
EMOTIONAL		
PHYSICAL		

COMMITMENT | STEWARD RESOURCES

GOALS	ACTION ITEMS	Q1 Q2 Q3 Q4
TIME		
TALENT		
MONEY		

ANNUAL PLAN | HIGH IMPACT HABITS

HABIT 1 | **ANNUAL PLANNING TIME**

Review: Every December, review the last year and then complete your Annual Plan for the coming year.

DATE COMPLETED	DATE REVIEWED

Quarterly accountability. Two important meetings need to happen every quarter.
1. Meet with your running buddy to review each other's Personal Plan.
2. Meet with your spouse (or running buddy if you are not married) to review your monthly financial budget.

PERSONAL PLAN REVIEW

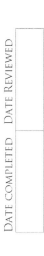

	Q1	DATE	Q2	DATE	Q3	DATE	Q4	DATE

BUDGET REVIEW

	Q1	DATE	Q2	DATE	Q3	DATE	Q4	DATE

HABIT 2 | **WEEKLY PLAN**

Establish a weekly time for planning, praying, and reviewing the prior week.

HABIT 3 | **DAILY EXECUTION**

Establish an everyday morning and evening routine.

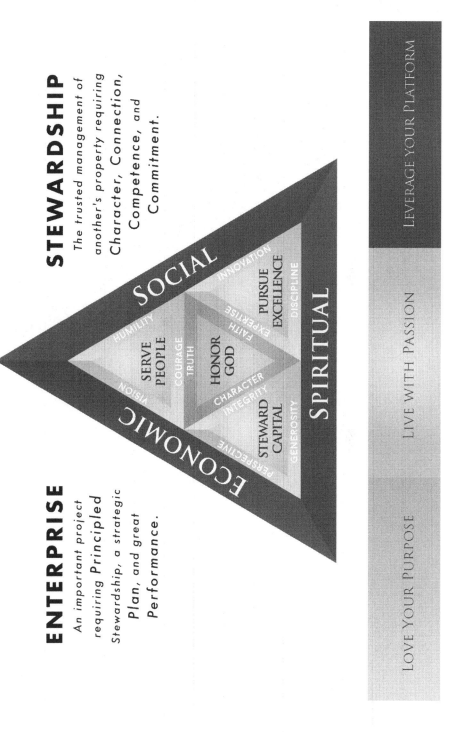

STEWARDSHIP

The trusted management of another's property requiring Character, Connection, Competence, and Commitment.

ENTERPRISE

An important project requiring Principled Stewardship, a strategic Plan, and great Performance.

SOCIAL

ECONOMIC

SPIRITUAL

INNOVATION

PURSUE EXCELLENCE

HUMILITY

FAITH

EXPERTISE

DISCIPLINE

SERVE PEOPLE

COURAGE
TRUTH

HONOR GOD

VISION

CHARACTER
INTEGRITY

STEWARD CAPITAL

PERSPECTIVE

GENEROSITY

LOVE YOUR PURPOSE

LIVE WITH PASSION

LEVERAGE YOUR PLATFORM

Notes

_____

_____

_____

_____

_____

_____

_____

_____

_____

_____

_____

_____

_____

_____

_____

_____

_____

Notes

_____

_____

_____

_____

_____

_____

_____

_____

_____

_____

_____

_____

_____

_____

_____

_____

_____

Notes

_____

_____

_____

_____

_____

_____

_____

_____

_____

_____

_____

_____

_____

_____

_____

_____

_____

_____

Notes

_____

_____

_____

_____

_____

_____

_____

_____

_____

_____

_____

_____

_____

_____

_____

_____

Notes

Notes

_____

_____

_____

_____

_____

_____

_____

_____

_____

_____

_____

_____

_____

_____

_____

_____

_____

Notes

_____

_____

_____

_____

_____

_____

_____

_____

_____

_____

_____

_____

_____

_____

_____

_____

Notes

_____

_____

_____

_____

_____

_____

_____

_____

_____

_____

_____

_____

_____

_____

_____

_____

_____

_____